D1444420

The Hitchhiker's Guide to the Galaxy

BY DOUGLAS ADAMS

BOOK ANALYSIS

By Tom O'Brien

Everything in this book is important (handwritten)

The Hitchhiker's Guide to the Galaxy

BY DOUGLAS ADAMS

Bright
Summaries.com

DOUGLAS ADAMS

ENGLISH AUTHOR, SCRIPTWRITER AND ESSAYIST

- **Born in Cambridge (England) in 1952.**
- **Died in Los Angeles in 2001.**
- **Notable works:**
  - *The Restaurant at the End of the Universe* (1980), novel (sequel to *The Hitchhiker's Guide to the Galaxy*)
  - *Dirk Gently's Holistic Detective Agency* (1988), novel
  - *Starship Titanic* (1998), video game

Douglas Adams was born in Cambridge, but spent a large portion of his childhood at an animal shelter run by his grandparents. He began writing creatively at an early age, and after attending Cambridge University, where he was a member of the well-known Footlights theatre group, he moved to London to write for television and radio. Apart from minor writing and acting roles for *Monty Python's Flying Circus*, his career

He was from Cambridge, England. He is an atheist.

was largely unsuccessful until he wrote the hugely popular *Hitchhiker's Guide to the Galaxy* radio series, which he later adapted to novel form, eventually extending the series to five books while also working as a writer and script editor for the BBC science-fiction television series *Doctor Who*. The success of the *Hitchhiker's Guide* meant that he was subsequently able to work on projects of his choosing. A notoriously slow and reluctant writer, he divided his time between infrequently publishing new books, working with animal conservation groups, assisting in the production of video games based on his work, and trying to get a film version of the *Hitchhiker's Guide* made. He died suddenly of a heart attack in Los Angeles in 2001.

As you read, identify and ~~markmark~~ mark quotatio
that could support
the theme and
genre. Include
the page number.

THE HITCHHIKER'S GUIDE TO THE GALAXY

Genre

A HUMOROUS SCIENCE FICTION NOVEL

- **Genre:** comedy science fiction
- **Reference edition:** Adams, D. (2002) *The Ultimate Hitchhiker's Guide to the Galaxy*. New York: Del Rey.
- **1st edition:** 1979
- **Themes:** philosophy, chance and probability, bureaucracy, computing

The Hitchhiker's Guide to the Galaxy is the first in a series of novels adapted from a comedy radio series written by Adams and broadcast in 1978. The story follows Arthur Dent, a stereotypical Englishman, as he is rescued from the destruction of the planet Earth by his friend Ford Prefect, an alien who has been stranded on Earth for the last fifteen years. After encountering Ford's cousin Zaphod Beeblebrox (a fugitive who is also the current President of the Galaxy), and Trillian, the only other survivor of the Earth's destruction, Arthur and Ford survive a series of absurd near-death experiences. *The Hitchhiker's Guide to the Galaxy*, a kind of electronic portable Encyclopaedia for which Ford is a researcher, provides both Arthur and the reader with the context in which the events of the story take place. The plot is continually driven forward by improbable coincidences, explained as side-effects of travelling in the *Heart of Gold*, a spaceship powered by an 'infinite improbability drive'.

Heart of Gold – include the name of the spaceship in your essay.

SUMMARY

ESCAPE FROM EARTH

important

Arthur Dent wakes up hungover in his house in a small English village. Suddenly remembering that his house is due to be demolished as part of a road construction project, he makes a last-ditch effort to prevent this. Arthur's friend Ford Prefect arrives with the double revelation that he is in fact an alien stranded on Earth, and that the planet, like Arthur's house, is scheduled for demolition as part of the construction of a "hyperspatial express route" (p. 36). Just as the demolition of Arthur's house begins, a huge fleet of spaceships crewed by Vogons – a race of aliens who dominate the 'Galactic Hyperspace Planning Council' – suddenly appear and use high-powered weapons to vaporize the Earth. Ford uses a device called an "electronic thumb" (p. 27) to hitch a lift on one of the spaceships from the fleet.

Meanwhile, 500 000 light-years away, the flamboyant, two-headed and three-armed President

Know Vogons

of the Galaxy Zaphod Beeblebrox arrives at the launch ceremony for the spaceship *Heart of Gold*, which is powered by an "infinite improbability drive" (p. 87), allowing it to cross the galaxy at huge speeds without using hyperspace. Using a bomb that immobilises everyone apart from himself and his companion Trillian, he carries out his plan of stealing the *Heart of Gold*.

While Arthur and Ford are still recovering from their teleportation to the Vogon ship, their presence is discovered by the captain. They are captured, and the Vogon captain tortures them by reading his own poetry aloud, which Arthur is able to understand through the 'Babel fish', a universal translator inserted into his ear. They survive the ordeal, but the Vogons throw them off the ship into deep space, unprotected. Just as they are about to asphyxiate, they are spontaneously picked up by the *Heart of Gold* as Zaphod and Trillian travel towards the Horsehead Nebula. On board, Arthur and Ford meet Marvin, a depressed robot, before the four humanoids discover with astonishment that not only are Ford and Zaphod related, but also that this is not the only connection between their lives.

Find out what the connection is

MAGRATHEA

When the ship reaches the nebula, Ford learns that Zaphod claims to have discovered the location of the legendary planet Magrathea, whose inhabitants supposedly created luxury, custom-made planets for the galaxy's richest citizens in the distant past. The planet's identity is confirmed when the *Heart of Gold* is attacked by an automated nuclear weapons system. The ship miraculously survives the attack, though Trillian's pet mice from Earth go missing, and the crew goes down to investigate the barren surface of the planet. When they discover an entrance to an underground tunnel system, Zaphod, Trillian and Ford investigate, leaving Arthur on the surface with only Marvin the robot for company.

As Trillian, Ford and Zaphod navigate the tunnel system, Zaphod attempts to explain his actions to the others. He reveals that the plot to steal the *Heart of Gold* and find Magrathea was devised by one of his predecessors as President of the Galaxy, with Zaphod agreeing to carry it out. Zaphod can't reveal the next step in the plan, or its ultimate goals, because this information is sealed in closed-off sections of his two brains, which can control his thoughts and actions, but which he cannot access directly. He, Trillian and Ford are gassed into unconsciousness before he can explain further.

DEEP THOUGHT AND THE ORIGINS OF THE EARTH

Meanwhile, to escape Marvin's constant complaints and self-pity, Arthur walks off from the tunnel entrance. He is startled when he almost walks into on old man, who does not seem surprised to find Arthur on the deserted surface of Magrathea, and takes him into the interior of the planet to visit the factory where custom planets were once created. The old man reveals that he is a Magrathean named Slartibartfast, and that the original Earth was created by the Magratheans for "hyper-intelligent pan-dimensional beings" (p. 171) who disguised themselves as mice in order to run the planet.

Arthur goes on to learn about the history of the beings who commissioned the construction of the Earth. Millions of years previously, they had created a supercomputer called Deep Thought in order to provide the answer to the question of "life, the universe and everything" (p. 177). After seven and a half million years, Deep Thought produced the cryptic answer "forty-two" (p. 188) and challenged its creators to explain exactly what their question actually was. Unable to do so, they asked Deep Thought to tell them what the question is. Deep Thought responded by offering to design an even more powerful computer, to be called Earth, to discover the exact nature of the question. Arthur learns from Slartibartfast that the Vogons destroyed the Earth five minutes before the end of this 'program'.

ESCAPE FROM MAGRATHEA

Slartibartfast takes Arthur to a conference room where he is reunited with Ford, Trillian and Zaphod. Also present are Trillian's white mice, who have revealed themselves as members of the pan-dimensional race who built Deep Thought and commissioned the Earth. They believe that, since he was present on Earth seconds before it was destroyed, Arthur might carry in his brain the "ultimate question" (p. 207) that solves the riddle of the answer forty-two. Thinking that the mice only need to scan Arthur's brain to discover the question, Ford and Zaphod are in favour of a lucrative deal, but when they discover that the mice plan to surgically remove Arthur's brain, they realise they must escape.

After incapacitating the mice's bodyguards, Ford, Zaphod, Trillian and Arthur make a run for the surface, only to be cornered by police who have finally caught up with Zaphod after his theft of the *Heart of Gold*. The two trigger-happy officers are on the verge of killing the group when their life-support systems mysteriously fail. Upon reaching the surface with the help of Slartibartfast, they find the police ship silent and inactive next to the *Heart of Gold*. Marvin, who remained on the surface while the others were below, reveals that he plugged himself into the police ship's computer and explained his view of the universe to it, causing it to commit suicide.

Aboard the *Heart of Gold* once more, Zaphod asks Arthur if he is hungry, and announces his plan to visit "the restaurant at the end of the universe" (p. 225).

the next book

CHARACTER STUDY

ARTHUR DENT

Arthur is a dark-haired man in his 30s who, before the destruction of the Earth, had moved out of London "because it made him nervous and irritable" (p. 6) to work at a local radio station in England's West Country. In some ways he is a stereotypical English man: he is introverted, "never quite at ease with himself" (*ibid.*), attaches huge importance to drinking tea, and is frequently sarcastic. Adams uses Arthur's reactions to the galaxy's advanced technology and revelations about Earth's 'true' history to provide much of the humour in the novel and its sequels.

Through the eyes of Ford and Zaphod, who are both well-seasoned men of the galaxy, Arthur often appears ignorant and dull-witted, having spent his life "far out in the uncharted backwaters of the unfashionable end of the western spiral arm of the galaxy"(p. 1), unaware that life existed outside the Earth. However, it is obvious that Ford also sees another side of Arthur's character, since he chose him as the only person he would rescue from the Earth's impending destruction, and Trillian defends him against Zaphod's spiteful remarks.

As he gets over the 'culture shock' of leaving Earth, Arthur displays some resourcefulness, such as pretending to admire the Vogon captain's terrible poetry, and coming up with the idea of switching on the infinite improbability drive to save the Heart of Gold and its crew from destruction by nuclear missiles. Arthur also manages to find dark humour in some of the shocking situations he is exposed to, and sometimes shows sympathetic understanding towards the other characters, despite their alien – from his point of view – nature.

FORD PREFECT

Ford Prefect is a long-term friend of Arthur's, who poses as an unsuccessful actor on Earth, but is in fact an alien from "a small planet in the vicinity of Betelgeuse" (p. 12). He is described as a normal-looking man - "not conspicuously tall, his features were striking, but not conspicuously handsome" (*ibid.*) - apart from the fact that "there was something ever so slightly odd about him" (*ibid.*). His real job is researching various planets for the encyclopaedic *Hitchhiker's Guide to the Galaxy*, but he has been stranded on Earth for 15 years after only intending to visit for a week, adopting an eccentric lifestyle and drinking heavily. He is fond of the humans who live on Earth but "remained desperately worried about the terrible number of things they didn't know about" (p. 50). This shows in his attitude towards Arthur, which is both protective and condescending.

Ford is a seasoned traveller of the galaxy, and this enables him to find a way for him and Arthur to escape the Earth's destruction. When they are rescued by the *Heart of Gold*, Ford has mixed feelings about being reunited with Zaphod; he is excited about 'knocking about' with his cousin and thinks it will be fun, but the two-headed man's manic behaviour both annoys and worries him. This tension between Ford's hedonism and his genuine concern for his friends and the state of the universe is developed further in later books in the series.

ZAPHOD BEEBLEBROX

Zaphod Beeblebrox is Ford's cousin who became President of the Galaxy during Ford's exile on Earth, and seems to take great delight in his celebrity status and the controversies he causes. He has two heads and a surgically implanted extra arm. He is extremely vain and conceited, but also very self-aware, saying to Trillian "if there's anything more important than my ego around, I want it caught and shot now" (p. 102). He is highly intelligent, but also ignorant about things that do not concern him directly, forgetful and insensitive, especially towards Trillian and Arthur.

Although he is from Betelgeuse, Zaphod displays several characteristics that reflect stereotypes about Americans (which are particularly common in British culture). He refers to Trillian as "honey (p. 45), Arthur as "kid" (p. 139) and says "hey" frequently. He is also displays unlimited self-confidence and ambition, which acts as a foil to Arthur's reserved, self-conscious 'Englishness', and leads to mutual distrust.

Zaphod's motives, which lead the group to the planet Magrathea, are partially unknown even to himself, having been concealed in sealed-off areas of his two brains. This aspect of Zaphod's character may well reflect Adams' writing technique, where stories were developed as he wrote with minimal pre-planning; Zaphod does not know where he is going next because, at the time of writing, neither did Adams.

TRILLIAN/TRICIA MCMILLAN

Trillian, or Tricia McMillan as she is known to Arthur, is an astrophysicist from Earth who escaped from the planet with Zaphod six months before its destruction, from a party at which Arthur was also present. She is described by Zaphod as having "ridiculously brown eyes" (p. 45) and by Arthur as "beautiful, charming, devastatingly intelligent" (p. 113). As a consequence of her early escape and her superior intelligence, she is much less bewildered than Arthur by the bizarre nature of the Galaxy and the events of the story. Like Ford, Trillian finds Zaphod's company entertaining but also exasperating, and feels a responsibility to help Arthur overcome his confusion and disorientation.

One possible criticism of the novel is that the character of Trillian is somewhat underdeveloped compared to the three male protagonists, as she contributes significantly less to the novel's abundant dialogue and plays a smaller role in moving the plot forward. This is corrected later in the series, with Trillian taking a much more central role in the third and fifth instalments, but it is also worth noting that all of the artificial intelligence systems in the novel are presented as male, and that the majority of the minor characters are also men.

MARVIN

Marvin is a robot who is present on board the *Heart of Gold* when it is stolen by Zaphod and Trillian, and is one of a pair of sentient artificial intelligences on the ship along with the computer, Eddie. He is the result of a failed experiment by the Sirius Cybernetics Corporation to give its robots "Genuine People Personalities" (p. 97). Instead of a balanced character, Marvin has been cursed with tremendous analytical intelligence along with intensely morbid depression, leading him cause a ship's computer to commit suicide just by talking to it. Marvin shares many characteristics with Eeyore, the donkey friend of A. A. Milnes's Winnie-the-Pooh and Piglet.

Radio:

Only voices + sound
nothing to see
Characters are
develped from other
characters talking
about them and
what they say about
themselves.

ANALYSIS

important to know

ORIGINS AS A RADIO COMEDY

The Hitchhiker's Guide to the Galaxy originated as a radio comedy that was broadcast on BBC Radio 4 in the UK in 1998. Although a lot the novel's content differs substantially from the radio series, the style of writing in the novel is clearly influenced by the original format.

This influence is most obvious in the dialogue between the characters, much of which remains mostly unchanged from the original scripts. The characters often engage in lengthy comical exchanges completely at odds with the life-threatening situations they find themselves in, such as when Ford attempts to convince a Vogon guard who is about to throw them off the ship into deep space that his job is essentially meaningless and he should consider alternative employment, when a Magrathean weapons system fires nuclear missiles at the *Heart of Gold*, and when galactic police officers are shooting at Ford, Arthur, Trillian and Zaphod. Also, much of the development of the characters, especially Arthur, happens through dialogue, which is more commonly associated with radio comedies and dramas than conventional novels and television series.

CULTURAL INFLUENCES: *DOCTOR WHO* AND MONTY PYTHON

The Hitchhiker's Guide to the Galaxy was not the first work to combine comedy with science fiction, but it was the first to achieve significant mainstream success. The author's links with two other British cultural phenomena provide the basis for interesting and separate comparisons of the science fiction and comedy elements in his work.

Adams worked as a script-writer and editor on the BBC television series *Doctor Who* (first aired in 1963) during the same period that he was writing the scripts for the *Hitchhiker's Guide* radio series. There are some significant similarities between the universes in the two works:

- Both *Doctor Who* and *The Hitchhiker's Guide* are located firmly on the 'soft' end of the science fiction spectrum, where technological devices, ships and weapons have spectacular capabilities which defy established laws of physics and plots are driven by highly improbable events. This is in contrast to 'hard' science fiction, in which writers strive to logically extrapolate new technologies from those that exist and stay within the known boundaries of physics.

- The spaceship *Heart of Gold* shares some abilities with the Doctor's vehicle the Tardis, such as crossing vast interstellar distances very quickly and having the ability to travel through time. Another famous feature of the Tardis – that it contains much more space than its outer dimensions suggest – is replicated by the planet Magrathea.

- Although Ford Prefect is depicted as considerably less heroic than the Doctor, there are some similarities between the two. Like the Doctor, Ford is an experienced and capable traveller of the Galaxy, and often educates Arthur about its more bizarre elements, just as the Doctor shares his knowledge with his various companions.

Although the style of *Doctor Who* is often playful and comedic, the sometimes surreal, sometimes satirical humour that is almost the defining feature of *The Hitchhiker's Guide to the Galaxy* is much more comparable to the work of the British sketch comedy group Monty Python, whose television series *Monty Python's Flying Circus* ran from 1969-1974, when Adams was in his late teens and early twenties. Adams was a member of the Footlights, the same theatre group where several members of Monty Python had met and collaborated, and later received writing credits and made minor appearances in the later episodes of the *Flying Circus*. Some comic and satirical elements are shared between *The Hitchhiker's Guide* and the work of Monty Python:

- *The Hitchhiker's Guide* opens with a satire of government bureaucracy, with the almost simultaneous destruction of Arthur's house and the entire planet Earth. Arthur finds the demolition plans "on display at the bottom of a locked filing cabinet in a disused lavatory with a sign on the door saying Beware of the Leopard" (p. 10), while the Vogon captain informs the Earth's population that the de-molition plans have been on display "only four light years away" (p. 37) on Alpha Centauri. Interactions between ordinary citizens and bureaucratic institutions were also regularly satirised in *Monty Python's Flying Circus*, and the way that Adams inserted commentary on contemporary politics into his galactic setting is similar to the way this was done with the historical settings of the Monty Python films *Monty Python's Life of Brian* (1979) and *Monty Python and the Holy Grail* (1975).

• Satire of philosophy and religion is another area where *The Hitchhiker' Guide* shows similarities to the work of Monty Python. Adams and the majority of the Python members were or are well-known atheists, and freely poked fun at religious beliefs, such as in the works of Adam's fictional author Oolon Colluphid, the writer of books such as *Who is this God Person Anyway?*, and *Monty Python's Life of Brian*, a satire of the life of Jesus Christ. Both *The Hitchhiker's Guide to the Galaxy* and Monty Python also place philosophers in unlikely scenarios, with Adams imagining philosophers forming a labour union to protest against Deep Thought's search for the meaning of life, and Monty Python having the philosophers of

Ancient Greece take on their modern German counterparts in a football match.

- As well as sharing the element of satire, *The Hitchhiker's Guide* and the work of Monty Python also share surrealist imagery and humour. The improbable landscape that Arthur and Ford find themselves in after being rescued by the *Heart of Gold* and the image of two nuclear missiles turning into a bowl of petunias and a sperm whale are strongly reminiscent of Terry Gilliam's surrealist animations for Monty Python. Both *The Hitchhiker's Guide* and the work of Monty Python are also reminiscent of the surreal imagery in Lewis Carroll's *Alice's Adventures in Wonderland* (1865), such as the smoking caterpillar and flamingo croquet.

THE BOOK WITHIN THE BOOK

The novel *The Hitchhiker's Guide to the Galaxy* takes its name from a fictional electronic book for which Ford Prefect is working as a researcher. Adams claims to have first thought of the idea when travelling in Austria in 1971 with a copy of a book called *A Hitchhiker's Guide to Europe*. As it is portrayed in the novel, 'The Guide' (as Ford

important to understand /

calls it) has evolved into a kind of universal encyclopaedia far beyond the scope of the traveller's
guide book that inspired it, and has "long since
supplanted the great *Encyclopaedia Galactica*
as the standard repository of all knowledge and
wisdom" (p. 4) in "more relaxed civilizations"
(*ibid.*). With the guide, Adams (writing in 1979)
seems to predict smartphone and tablet technology, as well as user-edited reference works like
Wikipedia.

At various points in the story, entries from
'The Guide' are used to replace the voice of the
narrator and supply both the reader and Arthur
Dent with background information about
elements of life in the Galaxy. For example,
Ford shows Arthur the entries for Vogons, the
Earth and Babel Fish as they recover from their
teleportation to the Vogon ship. Later in the
book, other entries give more details about the
size of the universe (p. 79), the Sirius Cybernetics
Corporation that built Marvin (p. 96), the planet
Magrathea (pp. 120-121) and a former business
partner of Zaphod's (pp. 154-155).

Far from using the neutral, unbiased language
used in real reference works, the Guide uses a

mix of dramatic, conversational and opinionated language, so that it is as much a home to Adams' comic voice as the dialogue between characters and the history of Deep Thought, as told to Arthur by Slartibartfast.

SCIENCE, TECHNOLOGY AND ARTIFICIAL INTELLIGENCE

As mentioned above, the science fiction of *The Hitchhiker's Guide to the Galaxy* is very 'soft', and only really limited by the imagination of the Author. This enabled Adams to advance and enhance the narrative in surprising ways, and maintain its comic aspects. However, this does not mean that the ideas behind some of the fictional scientific and technological ideas in the book lack sophistication, as Adams clearly thought deeply about some elements of technological development. The technologies in the book can therefore be divided into those with a light-hearted, comic purpose and those that, while still humorous, were used to make serious points.

Some examples of technologies in the book used for narrative or comic purposes are:

- The broadcast technology used by the Vogons to transmit the news of the Earth's impending destruction to its inhabitants, which produces "wonderful, perfect quadrophonic sound with distortion levels so low as to make a grown man weep" (p. 35).
- Ford's "sub-etha sense-o-matic" (p. 27) which enables him to detect the Vogon's approach, and his "electronic thumb" (*ibid.*) which lets him and Arthur hitch a lift on the Vogon ship.
- The "Poetry Appreciation Chairs" (p. 67) in which Ford and Arthur are strapped to be tortured by the Vogon Captain's compositions.
- Slartibartfast's "aircar" (p. 165) which enables Arthur to visit the interior of Magrathea, and later helps the group escape from the planet.
- The mouse-sized transport vehicles used by Trillian's white mice.
- The "Kill-o-zap" guns (p. 215) used by the police to attack the crew of the *Heart of Gold* as they try to escape Magrathea.

These devices lend the action a kind of 'B-movie' quality and conjure up the kind of pre-CGI visual styles of *Doctor Who* and *Star Trek*.

Other technologies in the book are the result of deeper and more serious thought about difficult scientific concepts and problems:

- The author uses the artificial intelligences in the story to make serious points about the ethics and limits of AI technology:
  - Marvin is clearly a sentient being, with intelligence that surpasses that of any human, but is treated as a menial worker by the human crew of the *Heart of Gold*. The well-meaning attempt to give him a human-like personality has backfired and caused him to suffer from morbid depression and the character could be read as a warning against the unintended consequences of technological development.
  - The computer Deep Thought delivers the answer 'forty-two' when asked the meaning of life, the universe and everything. Adams used Deep Thought to make the point that when AI surpasses humans in logical thinking, humans will not be able to follow the reasoning behind its conclusions, and that therefore technology will not be able to solve existential or ethical problems that are specific to human thought.

- The Sirius Cybernetics Corporation's products on the *Heart of Gold*, such as the cheerful doors, and "nutri-matic" drinks machine (p. 128), could be interpreted as a warning about the tendency of capitalism to use technological advances for trivial or entertainment purposes.
- The Babel Fish, although it is an organic lifeform, serves the technological purpose of being an instant, universal translator. The fictional Guide ends its entry with the point that "the poor Babel Fish, by effectively removing all barriers to communication, has caused more and bloodier wars than anything else in the history of creation" (p. 61). Here, Adams is making the point that as technology increases our superficial knowledge and understanding of different cultures, the lack of a corresponding increase in deeper understanding may well cause significant problems.

This juxtaposition of comic elements with serious ideas may well be what drives the continued popularity of *The Hitchhiker's Guide to the Galaxy* and its 'cult' status. As with any work of literature or other art forms, the quality of the ideas it explores and the artistic skill of its creator will ultimately decide whether it will someday come to be considered dated or continue to attract new readers.

We want to hear from you!
Leave a comment on your online library
and share your favourite books on social media!

[handwritten: understand thư answers to the questions]

FURTHER REFLECTION

[handwritten vertical: your opinion on the story, use examples from the story]

SOME QUESTIONS TO THINK ABOUT...

- The novelisation of *The Hitchhiker's Guide to the Galaxy* was adapted from a radio series, a reversal of the usual situation. Do you think it is well-suited to the novel format? Why, or why not?

- The plot of the novel is often driven forward by incredible coincidences. Do you find this style of storytelling enjoyable, or could it be considered 'lazy' writing on the part of the author?

[handwritten margin: choice]

- In the book, Arthur Dent is removed from his native environment and thrown into a universe he never knew existed. Do you know any other works of fiction (science fiction or otherwise) in which this happens to the central character? How do they compare?

- Marvin's intelligence seems to be directly proportional to how depressed he is. Do you think there is a relationship between high intelligence and depression?

- In the book, Zaphod is considered a good president, because "the job of Galactic President was not to wield power, but draw attention away from it" (p. 41). To what extent do you think this idea applies to presidencies in the real world?
- The fictional *Hitchhiker's Guide* is described as containing "much that is apocryphal, or at least wildly inaccurate" (p. 4). In your opinion, do reference works in the real world (e.g. Wikipedia) have this same problem? To what extent?

FURTHER READING

REFERENCE EDITION

- Adams, D. (2002) *The Ultimate Hitchhiker's Guide to the Galaxy*. New York: Del Rey.

ADDITIONAL SOURCES

- Gaiman, N. (2009) *Don't Panic: Douglas Adams & The Hitchhiker's Guide to the Galaxy*. London: Titan Books.

- Joll, N. ed. (2012) *Philosophy and The Hitchhiker's Guide to the Galaxy*. New York: Palgrave Macmillan.

ADAPTATIONS

- *The Hitchhiker's Guide to the Galaxy*. (2005) [Film]. Garth Jennings. Dir. USA/UK: Touchstone Pictures, Spyglass Entertainment, Hammer & Tongs, Everyman Pictures.

- *The Hitchhiker's Guide to the Galaxy*. (1984) [Video game]. Douglas Adams and Steve Meretzky. Infocom.

www.brightsummaries.com

Ebook EAN: 9782808012553

Paperback EAN: 9782808012560

Legal Deposit: D/2018/12603/383

Cover: © Primento

Digital conception by Primento, the digital partner of
publishers.

Made in the USA
Columbia, SC
26 June 2023